Contents

The Moon

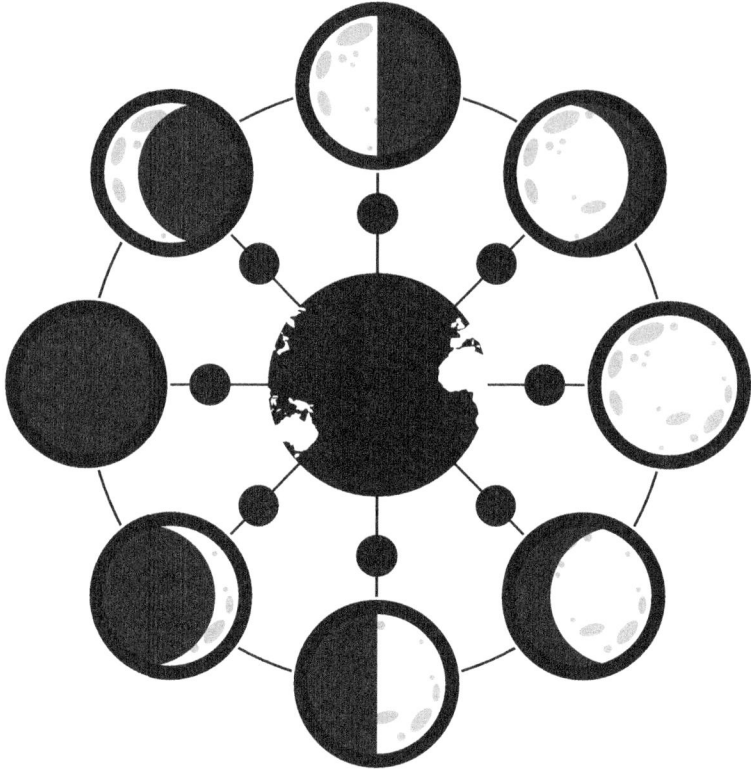

The Moon has an essential and nuanced part in magic and the occult.

A BRIEF HISTORY OF ASTROLOGY AND THE MOON

The Sumerians, who worshipped the gods of the Sun (Utu), Venus (Inanna), and the Moon, established the Moon's role in the astrological universe around 4000 BC (Nanna). Their rulers were descended from the priests who interacted with the gods.

Banu Priests, a rare type of priest that could discern the signs of the sky, appeared. These priests were foretelling natural events, generally a lunar eclipse.

IN MODERN WESTERN ASTROLOGY, THE MOON PLAYS AN IMPORTANT ROLE.

The Moon is a female influence in contemporary western astrology, defining childhood, maternal origins, and learned reactions. The Moon's position in relation to the other signs is thought to be very important. There is a sun sign and a moon sign for everyone. These indicate the position of the sun or moon in the zodiac at the moment of birth. The sun spends 30 days in each zodiac sign, whereas the moon goes through each sign once a month. Personality is determined by the sun, whereas emotions are determined by the moon. Your sun sign may tell you a lot about how you'll be seen in the world. The moon sign serves as a guide to the inner self's voice. Hopes, dreams, anxieties, insecurities, and intuitions are all associated with the moon sign.

IN INDIAN ASTROLOGY, THE MOON PLAYS AN IMPORTANT ROLE.

The Moon is known as Chandra in Indian Astrology. Chandra is the most powerful astral force, representing both intellect and body. Shipping, water items, pearls corals agriculture, and service under a woman are all connected with Chandra.

ALCHEMY AND MAGIC OF THE MOON

The Moon, whether male or female, is seen as having enormous power in astrology. Astrologers devote a portion of their work to anticipating how such force will affect human and earthly activity. Astrologers advise people to pay attention to the planets' ability to influence people to do things at specific periods when the stars are aligned in their favor. This invariably prompts debate about whether the same energy can be harnessed. At this time, astrology becomes magical.

The moon is a highly significant element in magic spells and ceremonial magic.

The Moon is related to moon magic. Many cultures believe that doing certain rituals during certain phases of the moon might bring about bodily or psychological change or transformation. The full moon and, to a lesser extent, the new moon have traditionally been the sites of these rites. Adherents of neopagan and witchcraft systems such as Wicca engage in such acts often. These beliefs appear to be in sync with many other cultures' customs, for example, the casting of the spell is frequently done at the full moon's pinnacle.

The enchantment of the changing seasons and the lunar cycle may be experienced with the aid of this helpful guide. by exploring the power and spells connected with each moon's seasonal and divine energies.

A GUIDE TO THE MOON'S EIGHT PHASES.

The various views or phases of the moon have been grouped into eight easy-to-understand descriptions that show how much of the Moon's daylight side is seen from Earth as the month passes.

- New moon
- The waxing crescent
- The first quarter
- The waxing gibbous
- The full moon
- The waning gibbous
- The last quarter
- The waning crescent

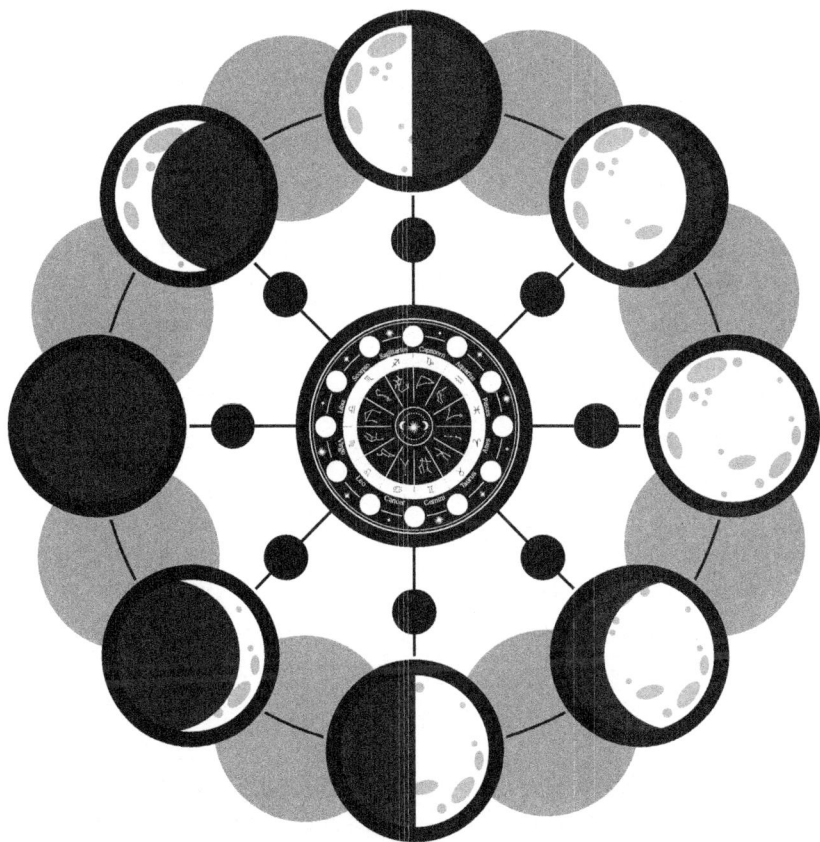

New Moon

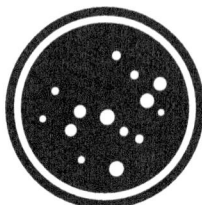

The New Moon is the first phase of the lunar cycle, beginning when the Moon returns in the night sky after a period of 2-3 days known as the 'Dark Moon.' It's a time for new beginnings, so it's excellent for creating goals and sowing seeds for the future. Allow your imagination to go wild as you create a new reality. This is an ideal time to take the first steps toward realizing your dreams.

The new moon signifies a new beginning. The moon is rarely visible during this phase, and the sky can appear black. With the moon out of sight, this is a good time to undertake shadow work or acknowledge our dark sides, or shadow selves, that we usually keep buried.

For example, perhaps you have a manipulative side that you deny exists when questioned. Is there any way you could use your skills in a healthy way, such as to advance in your job without harming others? Or, rather than controlling your partner, you may use your ability to read people to encourage them to interact together?

New moons are great for exploring our shadow sides and finding ways to work positively with them.

The new moon is also a great time to make goals and intentions for the future cycle, as new moons signify new starts. What do you hope to achieve in the coming month? Is there a toxic partner in your life that you're now ready to let go of in order to make place for the love of your life? The new moon is an excellent time to celebrate fresh beginnings, particularly in love. And you already know what starting over entails: letting go of the past. The new moon is on your side if you wish to eliminate negative energy from your love life in order to attract your ideal partner.

The black moon is brimming with possibilities; you don't have to know how things will play out; all you have to do is take action to get things started. Set intentions based on your deepest wishes, let go of fear, lean into faith, and trust your inner vision now.

KEYWORDS:
New beginnings, setting intentions, letting go, reboot, taking time for yourself, soul-searching.

RITUALS:
Take a bath to symbolize washing away the old
Meditate to create stillness
Re-decorate your altar
Journal
Set new intentions

TAROT:
The Fool

CRYSTALS:
Labradorite, black moonstone, iolite, tektite, obsidian, and transparent quartz are all good choices.

Waxing Crescent Moon

The Waxing Crescent Moon is the part of the lunar cycle when the Moon begins to increase. The energies are very magnetic, so it's an excellent time to do some constructive magic bringing in what you desire from life and reality, whether it's projects, goals, or emotional states and behaviors like increased self-love, compassion, a positive attitude, courage, and so on. The Waxing Crescent's energy is all about reaching within and drawing out what you want more of before thinking about and visualizing what you want to bring forth from the outside world.

The Moon brightens as she approaches fullness in her waxing crescent phase. What began in the new phase is beginning to take shape, as we can see. This stage demonstrates a dedication to one's goals. Establishing roots and laying a solid foundation takes time, work, and commitment. The process is still in its early phases, and letting go of old ideas and practices that stifle fresh growth is difficult. It's time to keep placing one foot in front of the other and moving forward.

KEYWORDS:
Manifesting, visualizations, affirmations.

RITUALS:
Guided visualization exercise
Create new affirmations
Celebrate success

TAROT:
The Magician

CRYSTALS:
Nuummite, rainbow moonstone, and emerald.

First Quarter Moon

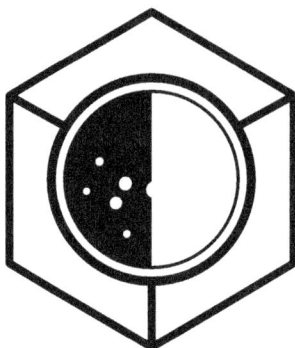

The First Quarter Moon is all about attracting from the outside world, but the New Moon is all about delving within and bringing out. It's the best time to do magic that draws things in, whether it's a person (lover, friend, client), success, money, or anything else. This is also an excellent opportunity to retrieve misplaced items.

The Moon is half full when she is in her first quarter phase. She's brilliant, yet we only get to glimpse a fraction of her. The process of actualizing goals and allowing plans emerge is symbolized by this midway point in the sky. It may take a push to keep going once you've gotten this far. This stage of the cycle need your undivided attention. You may not do everything perfect the first time, but until you try, you'll never know. The fresh visions you created under the new moon have reached the pinnacle of their creative potential. This is the moment to strive bravely for what you desire, in order to attract what you've asked for and more.

KEYWORDS:
Creativity, moving forward, motivation, resistance, navigating obstacles.

RITUALS:
Connect to dreams and visions
Release all judgment
Forgive oneself and others
Detailed intentions
Plan or schedule
Find inspiration

TAROT:
Strength or The Star

CRYSTALS:
Jet, onyx, and lapis lazuli.

Waxing Gibbous Moon

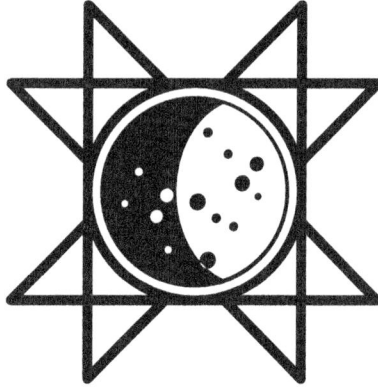

The energies of the Waxing Gibbous Moon, which are still in the 'constructive' magic phase, are great for giving anything you've been working on some more oomph. If you're having problems finishing a work or keeping to a schedule, use these energies to give you a boost and help you overcome temptations and opposition.

The Moon is nearly full now, and the mounting intensity is impressive. Before the final result is disclosed, this is your last chance to make adjustments. The waxing gibbous phase, like preparing to unveil a work of art, may be stressful. What if it isn't flawless? Now is the moment to remain focused and examine all of the details to see what needs to be reworked or adjusted in order to bring everything together. This accumulating energy may be relentless, so it's crucial not to become concentrated on unimportant details.

The waxing moon phase happens when the moon progresses from a new to a full moon, and it gets larger and brighter. During the waxing moon, the moon is rising, brighter, and providing an ideal time for sympathetic magic centered on development.

Sympathetic magic is defined as magic that works via symbolic resemblance. The moon is shining brightly, therefore let's use it to improve your career, self-esteem, and love life.

KEYWORDS:
Refinement, perspective, alignment, trust, action, high energy.

RITUALS:
Read affirmations daily
Welcome the support of the universe

TAROT:
The Wheel of Fortune

CRYSTALS:
Fluorite, carnelian, and citrine.

Full Moon

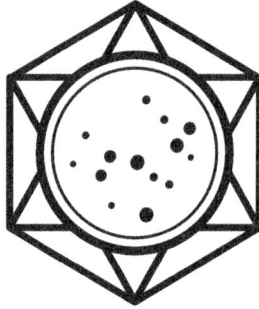

The Full Moon phase is the most potent in the lunar cycle, and hence the best time to handle major difficulties or obstacles you may be facing. Concentrate your spells and rituals on the things that are most important to you. This is also an excellent period for magic and meditations centered on psychic growth, spirituality, and divination.

On full moons, emotions run high, and everything is extra intense. You can utilize this intensity to cast almost any spell you want, safe in the knowledge that you'll be aided by a dazzling ball of flashing power. During full moons, many people charge their crystals by setting them somewhere where they would be exposed to light. Another trick is to make full moon water by placing a glass of water on top of a letter of intent under the light of the full moon. Allow the full moon to charge the water before using it.

Any magic can be done with additional intensity under a full moon, but it's also a period when psychic talents are enhanced. When the Moon is full, we see her in all of her glory, and it's the only time we get to view her completely. The full phase is a metaphor for completeness and satisfaction. This is the manifestation phase! We establish intentions while the Moon is new. We give birth to our creations when she is full. Whatever you've been working on for a long time is about to be uncovered in the light of consciousness. This is the climax of the entire waxing cycle's outcomes. It's time to stomp your feet and give thanks joyfully to the cosmos and to yourself.

KEYWORDS:
Celebrate, gratitude, reflection, expansion.

RITUALS:
Write a gratitude list
Bathe in the moonlight
Celebrate the past two weeks
Show gratitude to the moon
Attend a moon circle

TAROT:
The Sun

CRYSTALS:
Moonstone, selenite, and quartz.

Waning Gibbous Moon

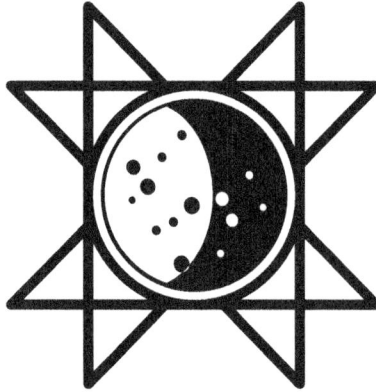

After the Full Moon, we enter the 'waning phase,' when energies are more favorable to rejecting, banishing, and removing what is unwelcome. During this phase, perform spells and rituals aimed towards minor banishings and cleansings, whether literally or in terms of putting an end to something that hasn't worked in a long time. This is a good time to reflect and clarify what is no longer in line with your objectives in order to determine what they are.

With the full moon, the declining phase began, and the Moon is already plainly retreating. This phase is also referred to as "disseminating," implying the necessity of sharing the outcomes of your work with the rest of the world. How are your manifestations assisting and providing a purpose for others? In addition, the waxing phase's creative endeavor left some cleanup to be done. It's time to accept responsibility for yourself and your achievements, to connect with the cycle's deeper knowledge, and to anchor the energies. As you collect materials to begin the descent of the complete moon cycle, express appreciation to your elders and ancestors and ask for their assistance.

The waning moon is the time between a full moon and a new moon when the moon grows dimmer. According to sympathetic magic, this waning moon is good for banishing work or cutting links with a previous partner. Casting charms to rid oneself of feelings for someone you know is toxic for you, uncertainty, or self-doubt are among the most effective banishing work you can undertake. Get rid of whatever bad energy you may have. Those beliefs that imply you are deserving of bad luck. Discrimination in the workplace must be eliminated.

KEYWORDS:
Release, receive, appreciate, abundance.

RITUALS:
Release negative energy
Burning ritual
Meditate on receiving

TAROT:
The Tower

CRYSTALS:
Calcite, angelite, and unakite jasper.

Last Quarter Moon

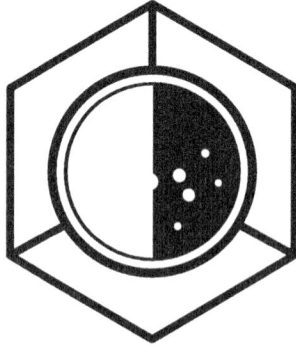

The declining half moon is the last quarter phase. It represents our growing awareness of who we are and what we've made in the world. Because the end is approaching, it might feel like a catastrophe.

There isn't much time left to modify the end result, which encompasses the outcomes of our efforts, their far-reaching influence, and all we've learnt as a result of them. As we surrender to be reborn, the fading moon will take control, metaphorically dissolving our illusions of reality. The last quarter moon depicts those times when you finally have a sense of the larger picture. If you're prepared to let go of previous ties in order to make way for the future, there's a lot of possibility for vision and prophesy.

This is the declining final quarter when we see half of the moon in the sky again. This is the moment to let go of bad feelings and submit. Make a list of positive affirmations. Before the next dark moon and beginning the cycle all over again, it's a perfect opportunity to write and check in with what's worked/happened.

KEYWORDS:
Make space, set boundaries, breathe.

RITUALS:
Protection rituals
Space cleansing
Breathwork

TAROT:
Judgement

CRYSTALS:
Rose quartz, bronzite, and sodalite

Waning Crescent Moon

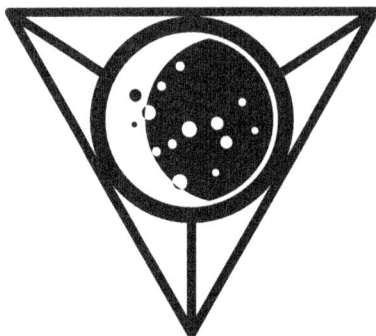

Endings, including the creation of new beginnings, contain immense magic. The Moon is near the conclusion of her cycle when she reaches the declining crescent. It's time to let go of what you don't need and to do it gracefully. Be aware of the emptiness that lies ahead, and know that it will ultimately fill. The Veil thins during this period, making it easier to receive messages and signals.

You learn the bigger truths of existence by leaning into faith and appreciating the darkness inside and without. You are compelled to make sacrifices for future generations, including your own rebirth, during this time. Service, love, and compassion are all ways to leave your best self behind.

The black moon occurs when the moon is so little that it is scarcely visible in the sky. It is the ending that generates the beginning. This is the lunar cycle's lowest energy phase, and it will be the most emotional. It's a moment to turn inside and withdraw from life in order to examine your deepest emotional levels. Accept your worries and fears and consider what they're trying to teach you.

Consider what you no longer desire in your life. Take lengthy, hot showers and treat yourself with kindness at this period.

KEYWORDS:

Recuperate, self-care, recharge, surrender, reflect.

RITUALS:

Deep reflection

Close loose ends and complete projects before the new moon

TAROT:

Justice

CRYSTALS:

Black tourmaline, petalite, and obsidian

Lunar Eclipses

Every 29.5 days, both moon and sun are in the same degree of the astrological sign when a new moon occurs. However, the sun and moon will eclipse each other roughly 2-5 times every year. Because the sun and moon are either together or directly apart, the energy is stronger.

Eclipses can be classified into three categories. When the moon passes through only the outside borders of the earth's shadow, or penumbra, a penumbral eclipse occurs it's frequently quite mild, and many people don't even notice it. Section of the moon passes through the earth's umbra, which is the more direct, centered part of the shadow, during a partial eclipse. We may often see the moon in the sky during a partial eclipse since the earth, sun, and moon do not form a direct line during this occurrence.

When the earth's shadow totally blocks the moon and it gets

entirely black for a length of time, we observe a total eclipse. During the occurrence, the moon frequently seems to have a crimson or bloodlike tint. Many people imagine this when they hear the words "lunar eclipse," and it has long been a forerunner of big events in many civilizations.

Some practitioners consider the eclipse period which is usually rather brief to be the equivalent of a full moon cycle compressed into a single event. After all, during an eclipse, the moon appears to be waxing, waning, and reappearing.

A lunar eclipse is seen as a metaphysical bonus round in certain modern magical traditions, meaning that any spellwork performed at this time is enhanced and has a bit more force behind it.

Because an eclipse only happens during the full moon phase of the lunar cycle, it's an excellent time to undertake personal growth and spiritual development practices. Some instances include, but are not limited to, the following:

- Increase your intuitive awareness and psychic abilities, as well as divination and wisdom, with these spells.

- Healing rituals or magic, especially those involving women's secrets or reproductive health.

- Drawing Down the Moon or other spell work meant to evoke the god or goddess of your tradition are examples of rituals that connect you directly with divinity.

- Any work that is relevant to the development of your magical abilities.

- Rituals honoring the gods and goddesses of the moon now is a great time to make a sacrifice to them!

The Seven Days of the Week

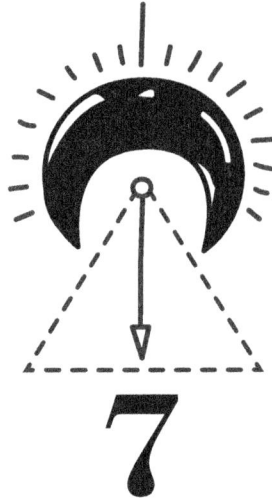

Sunday-Sun: Mental and physical health management. Problem-solving insight and divine communication Compassionate magic, ritual, and tradition.

Monday-Moon: Divination techniques, invocations and evocations, innovation and projects, divine & spiritual communications, healing, grounding, centering, and home protection.

Tuesday-Mars: Fertility spells, self-protection, glamours, confidence, hexes, doll work, and jinxing.

Wednesday Mercury: Luck and success; profession, hobbies, travels, love, and events in the near future.

Thursday-Jupiter: Spiritual and personal growth, health, and a mind, body, and soul emphasis. Exercise, food, and self-judgment.

Friday-Venus: Forgiveness, tying knots, glitz and glam, and blood. Place a higher priority on people and the environment than on yourself. Various types of beautification.

Saturday-Saturn: Getting rid of negativity and putting a stop to things. Control, enticement, and domination, charm When is the best moment to stop or stop harmful effects or influences with the intention to stop them

The Influence of Zodiac Signs on Moon Magic

Keep the Moon's zodiac sign and phase in mind while executing a ceremony. Each zodiac sign is related with a different Earth element and has its own set of traits that may be used to your advantage.

The indications and energy imprints listed below can be used in your practices.

ARIES
Mars rules Aries, a fire sign that governs initiative, activity, and urges. Protection rituals or rituals for dominance, power, strength, passion, and lust are ideal at this time.

TAURUS
Taurus is an earth sign controlled by Venus, and it is the best time to undertake rituals related to money and relationships. Rituals done at this period may be highly successful and yield great long-term benefits due to Taurus' intransigence.

GEMINI
Gemini is an air sign with a dualistic character that may make regulating the course of your spells and magic challenging. It does, however, provide a fantastic chance for rituals centered on creativity, new ideas, and travel. Just be cautious and mindful of its changing characteristics.

CANCER
Cancer, a water sign associated with sentiments, is an excellent period for rituals linked to family, domestic life, and reproduction.

LEO
Leo is a fire sign, and its energy is ideal for casting spells and using magic to help you advance in your work, courage, and leadership.

VIRGO
Virgo, an earth sign ruled by Mercury, has a strong mental influence, making this the ideal time to undertake rituals that need a lot of attention to detail. Cast rituals centered on health, healing, and education with the energies of the Moon in Virgo.

LIBRA
Libra's energies are ideal for balancing any life's extremes. When conducted under the Libra Moon, rituals involving relationships, partnerships, and romance can be particularly productive.

SCORPIO

When the Moon is in Scorpio, it is the best time to work with psychic abilities, divination, and advanced rituals. The sign of Scorpio is especially favorable to casting fertility charms due to its intense sexual energies.

SAGITTARIUS

Sagittarius, the fire sign, has a particularly strong intellectual effect, which may be useful for casting charms and rituals for legal concerns, truth, education, and protection.

CAPRICORN

Capricorn's steady earth energies, while not as adamant as Taurus', are ideal for performing magic involving organization, stability, and ambition.

AQUARIUS

The Moon's energies in Aquarius are ideal for performing friendship spells, conquering addictions, and developing psychic talents.

PISCES

It is best to do Mental Magic, such as telepathy, clairvoyance, lucid dreaming, divination, and contact with spirits, when the Moon enters the sign of Pisces.

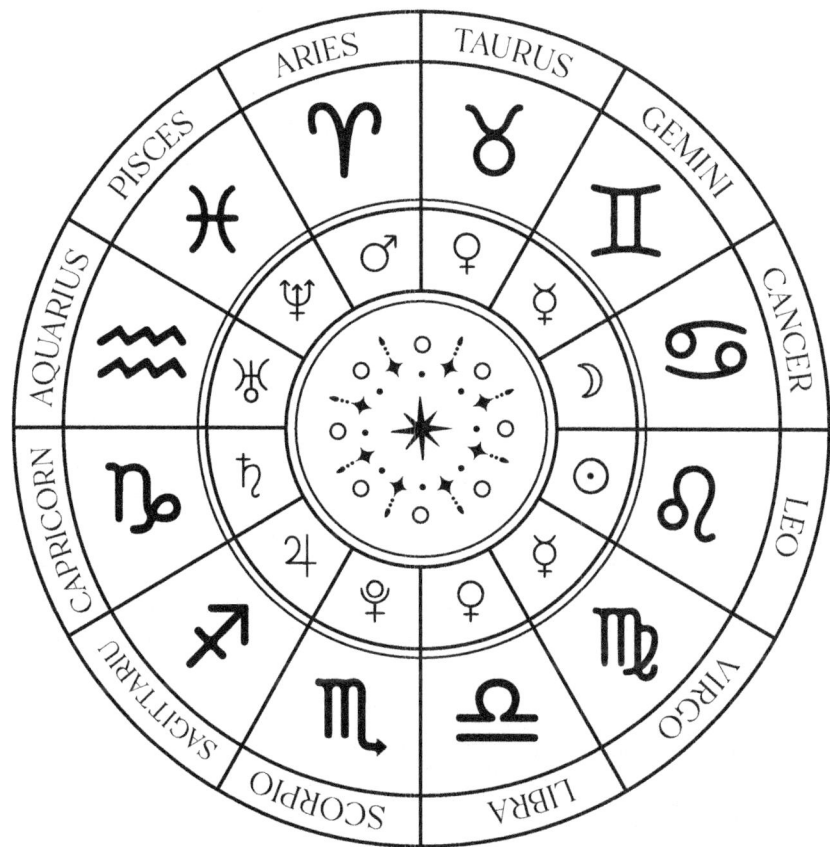

The Full Moon in Astrology Signs

The Moon controls the Water-ruled sign of Cancer and people born between June 21st and July 22nd in Western Astrology. Cancerians are nice, smart, tenacious, and temperamental, yet they may be fickle at times. Cancerians are very sensitive and caring. Those born under the sign of the Crab value their home, comfort, and safety. Cancerians are sentimental people who despise confrontation and criticism.

When the Full Moon enters their zodiac sign on the celestial Wheel, its energies affect their attitude, thoughts, feelings, and decisions, not only those born under Cancer's reign. The Full Moon's transit creates tremendous and different vibrations of influence by forming various aspects with other planetary bodies and the Sun. Below, you can see how the Moon's pull varies as it moves through the twelve zodiac signs:

FULL MOON IN ARIES: The Moon's energy stimulates impulsivity and excitement, yet it may also lead to conflict and hubris. It's a time of self-assurance, self-expression, and self-discipline as the Full Moon enters Aries. Emotional health, setting boundaries, artistic interests, and new projects are all important.

FULL MOON IN TAURUS: The energy effect is earthy, loving, and ardent. The Moon emphasizes the importance of emotional foundation, centering, and stability. The fundamental theme is a love of all things creative and an appreciation for beauty.

FULL MOON IN GEMINI: The energies of the Full Moon add to the period's unpredictability and volatility. Fickleness, restlessness, and plenty of energy are all factors. A greater demand for intellectual stimulation and learning activities exists.

FULL MOON IN CANCER: The planetary vibrations emphasize familial ties, friendships, and romantic relationships, with an emphasis on home. Compassion, nurturing, and deepening existing bonds are now essential. However, moodiness, emotional bewilderment, and uncertainty accompany the period.

FULL MOON IN LEO: When the Full Moon enters Leo, it is all about gaining attention, adulation, and limelight. Friendships flourish, and the energies emphasize rewards for hard effort or recognition for your distinctive qualities.

FULL MOON IN VIRGO: With the Moon in Virgo, all situations requiring concrete facts, reasoning, analysis, and commerce take center stage. The era is characterized by purity, clarity, and simplicity. Emotional expression and inquiry are now less supported by the energies.

FULL MOON IN LIBRA: Finding balance, harmony, and peace of mind in all aspects of your life is essential. However, because Libra is an Air sign, maintaining harmony may be a continual battle. Highlights include chattiness, intellectual stimulation, and socializing.

FULL MOON IN SCORPIO: When the Moon enters Scorpio, ecstasy, exhilaration, jealousy, love, and hatred become more strong. Neurosis and obsession become actual possibilities as a result of the intensity of emotion. In emotional concerns, cynicism, skepticism, hesitancy, indecisiveness, and great caution reign.

FULL MOON IN SAGITTARIUS: This is a time of optimism, hope, taking risks, and adventure. Spiritual and intellectual enlightenment are hot topics right now. The Moon in Sagittarius stimulates a drive to try new things or perceive existing things in fresh ways.

FULL MOON IN CAPRICORN: When the Moon is in Capricorn, orderliness, levelheadedness, strength, and constancy reign supreme. Unless non-conformity helps to improve order, tradition currently reigns supreme. Patience and endurance are emphasized, and all business-related pursuits take center stage.

FULL MOON IN AQUARIUS: When the Moon enters Aquarius, the energy is one of liberation from convention, boldness, and eccentricity. The emphasis is on individuality, freedom, and resistance. The impact of this time is marked by shifts in perception, abrupt transformations, and the unexpected.

FULL MOON IN PISCES: With the Moon in Pisces, there will be a greater emphasis on spiritual pursuits, inner journey work, and self-exploration. Dreamwork, visions, spiritual journeys, meditation, and experiencing altered levels of consciousness are among the hallmarks of the program. The period is marked by imagination, fantasy, and nostalgia.

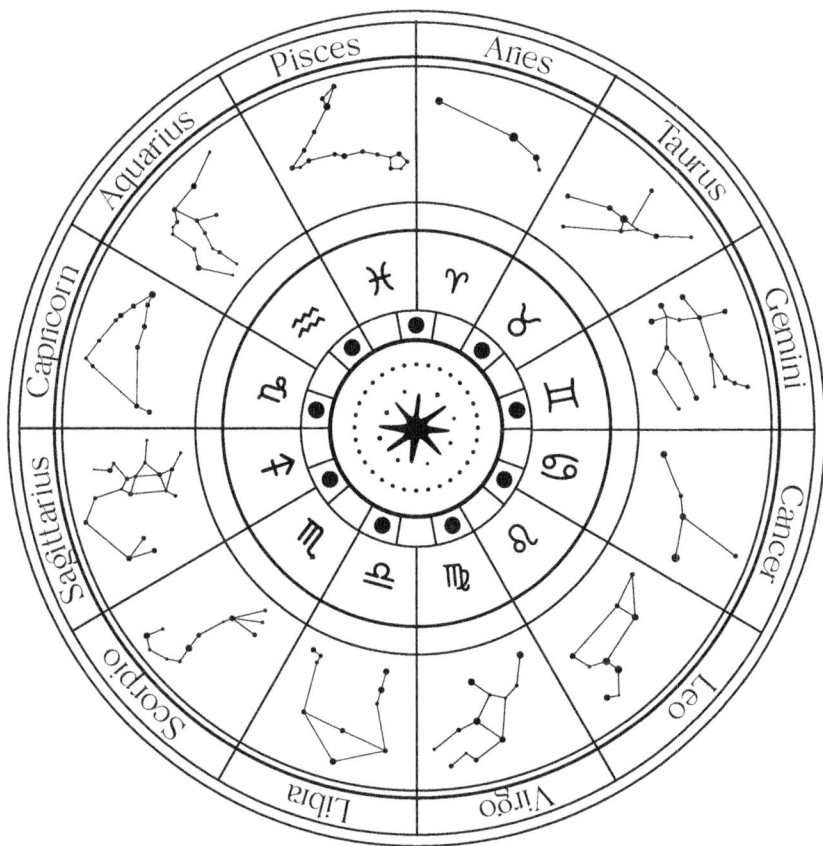

The Year's Moons

A full Moon occurs once a month. A blue Moon occurs when there are two full Moons in the same month. A blue Moon appears once a year on the calendar. The Moons of each month were given various names by ancient cultures. To represent what the Moon meant to them in a particular month, different cultures gave it different names. Some of the Moon names make sense, but others may not unless you understand the rationale behind them.

JANUARY
Name: Wolf Moon

The Wolf Moon is the full moon in January. When the earth and water have become as hard as stone due to the cold, this is a place of tremendous quiet. The term for this month's full moon stems from long-ago Algonquian observations that wolves howl in hunger when food becomes scarce during the January evenings. The Hunger Moon, the Old Moon, the Moon after Yule, and the Cold Moon are some of the other names for this moon.

It's a period of waiting, endurance, and survival, but there's a lot of promise in the works. Consider the trip through the seasons that awaits you this coming year. The path spreads out in front of you like a blanket of freshly fallen snow. That's exactly what you've been looking for. Point zero is the Wolf Moon. The new beginning. Because the gift of a second opportunity only comes around once a year, you want to be deserving of such a glorious start. Before you can dedicate yourself to your spiritual journey for the year ahead, you must start from a place of emptiness and purity.

So now is the time to execute banishing rituals to cut links with any negative energy or unpleasant memories from the previous year that you fear may follow you. During this season of cold, emptiness, and potential, you should also cast protective charms to strengthen your psychic and physical vitality. Finally, this is a fantastic time to use Tarot, runes, Ogham, pendulum, scrying, or your chosen means of divination to glean insights into the year's possibilities.

Alternative Name: Old Moon
The start of a new year calls for cleansing and regeneration; it's a time to start over, wash away the old, and make fresh beginnings.

Spellwork inspiration: Cast or recast a protection spell on your house, recite a unique protection charm for yourself and the people you love, or conduct a protection charm on a specific object that may be essential to you in the new year. Use salt and common herbs like rosemary, basil, cinnamon, or mint to make a protection jar or sachet. Place Black Obsidian, your go-to protection stone, in your magic pouch as well. Use a black bag for your sachet or include a wolf, fox, or coyote charm to invoke some of the Wolf Moon's correspondences.

Crystals to carry with you: Garnet, Hematite, or Selenite

FEBRUARY

Common Name: Storm Moon

The Storm Moon is the full moon in February. This is a harsh, windy time of year when the snow might come back with a fury. The term for this month's full moon stems from Algonquian observations that heavy snowstorms usually occur in February. The Quickening Moon is another name for this moon. As the Imbolc sabbat commemorates, February is a month of new beginnings and regeneration. You desire to clear both mental and physical clutter this month to create room for new endeavors. Try a purification ritual and cast spells for health and vigor on this full moon night.

Alternative name: Hunger Moon

With winter's supplies exhausted, the need for spring is a spiritual as well as a physical hunger.

Spellwork inspiration: Declutter your space, eliminate everything that isn't helping you feel good and undertake a thorough Spring cleaning. Then clear the energy in your environment. Say a cleaning chant, spray your space with water mixed with salt, rosemary, and essential oil, or clean with smoke. Please don't buy white sage bundles unless you're Indigenous; instead, consider a more sustainable herb bundle like lavender, cedar, or rosemary!

Charge your crystals in Full Moon snow and say hello to animal companions like chickadees to include the Hunger Moon's magical correspondences.

Crystals to carry with you: Amethyst or Jasper

MARCH
Name: Worm Moon

After the worm tracks that appeared in the recently thawed earth, Native Americans named this last full moon of winter the worm moon. After the tapping of the maple trees, the moon is also known as chaste moon, death moon, crust moon, and sap moon.

Alternative Name: Sap Moon

March is a month of uncertainty, seasonal shifts, and surges of energy for Wiccans. The sap in the trees is increasing, and the spring equinox is approaching. Your forthcoming endeavors must be chosen, organized, and blessed. Perform a blessing ceremony and fertility magic on the night of the full moon. March, as they say, is a month that comes in like a lion and goes out like a lamb. Consider the weather extremes that are common in March to understand this phrase. Snowstorms that appear straight out of the depths of winter are not unusual at the beginning of the month, but the month's end can herald some pleasant and mild weather that provides a nice peek of the beginning of summer. March is a month marked by polar opposites, upheaval, and quick change. All of this spiritual force is reflected in the Sap Moon, the full moon of the month, and you may use it to fuel your magic work.

Spellwork inspiration: Fill a sachet with seeds and household herbs like cinnamon or basil, as well as things that reflect what you're attempting to develop or materialize (ideally in a green bag to represent the Moon's color connection). If you're looking for new career success or fortune, a few pennies would be enough. On this day, sow seeds in your garden or buy a new houseplant to indicate growth and new life, and use thyme to represent one of the Worm Moon's many magical correspondences.

Crystals to carry with you: Bloodstone, Kambaba Jasper, or Citrine

APRIL
Name: Pink Moon
Native Americans used the April Full Moon to depict the hue of wild ground phlox. One of the first flowers to bloom this month is the phlox. Walking beneath the Full Moon while admiring the first spring flowers, regardless of hue, is a magical experience!

Alternative name: Seed Moon
April is the time to sow the seeds of your projects. March's erratic weather is giving way to more steady warmth and pleasant temperatures. Spring is on its way to becoming early summer. You may still need to be cautious when it comes to protecting sensitive baby seedlings (particularly if those seedlings are real plant seedlings), but the moment has come to sow those seeds and nurture your projects as they sprout under the Seed Moon's light.

Spellwork inspiration: Make a sachet (in a pink bag, of course!) with items you already have around the house for motivation and productivity when starting a new project, including salt, stones like Carnelian and Tiger's Eye for creativity and strength, and common herbs like cinnamon for success or even coffee for motivation. Consider selecting a chant that connects with you and your objectives, or writing a more personal chant for bravery that you can repeat three times if you need courage to make a change.

Crystals to carry with you: Garnet, Rose Quartz, or Lapis Lazuli

MAY
Name: Flower Moon
After the rains and winds of April have passed, the sun begins to warm the land, allowing us to sow the gardens. May is traditionally the month when we start sowing our crops. Get out in the garden and dig your hands into the dirt beneath a Flower Moon. May is a fiery month, full of fire and passion, and spring

is a season of fertility. It's also known as the Hare Moon Month, because we all know what hares get up to in the spring. A large bonfire ceremony will be held once the sun has set.

This is an excellent time to focus on career and job-related magic. Are you considering changing jobs or pursuing a career in a different field? Do you want to take a class or earn a degree? Allow the seeds that you sowed last month to sprout and thrive in your favor. This month, use fire divination to help you find your way. Here are some things you can do this month to help us lay the seeds for future success.

Alternative name: Milk Moon
The full moon in May is known in English as the Milk moon, in Algonquian as the Flower moon, in Hindi as Buddha Poornima, and in Sinhala Buddhism as Vesak Poya.

Spellwork inspiration: Take a self-love ritual bath to celebrate yourself. Rose petals, diluted lavender or ylang-ylang oil, Epsom salts, or a bath bomb containing any of these components are also good options. Light some pink, white, and/or yellow candles and surround the bathtub with Rose Quartz and Rhodonite, the ultimate self-love stones. While soaking in the Flower Moon's energies, repeat a self-love mantra to yourself!

Crystals to carry with you: Malachite, Unakite, or Rhodonite

JUNE
Name: Mead Moon
The sun has taken over in June, and the fields are flourishing. Juno, the Roman goddess of marriage, is honored in this month, which also marks the beginning of Litha, the summer solstice. In many traditional traditions, the full moon this month is known as the Strong Sun Moon, but it's also known as the Lover's Moon, the Honey Moon, or the Strawberry Moon. This time of year is linked with the woodpecker in various Native American belief systems.

Because the evenings are short in June, it's an excellent time to take use of solar energy, and the full moon is frequently visible in the sky before the sun sets. Take advantage of this by staying outside later than usual and embracing the combined power of the sun and moon. Sun and moon, masculine and feminine, day and night - it's a beautiful balance of opposites and equilibrium.

This is the month when magical workings are best for preserving and improving what you already have.

Alternative name: Strawberry Moon
Strawberry season peaks in this month, which Europeans dubbed the Rose Moon.

Spellwork inspiration: Under the June Full Moon, dream magic is your ally. However, dream interpretation is not something that can be learned in a single night. Even recalling one's dreams might be challenging for some people. June is the perfect time to start a dream notebook if you've always wanted to. You might also make a dream sachet or use a dream tea to keep under your pillow. Amethyst, for opening the third eye, and Moonstone, for dream recall, are two stones that go well with dreamwork. Lavender, thyme, chamomile, and rosemary, as well as the more difficult-to-find vervain and mugwort, are all dreamy herbs.

Of course, you'll want to eat strawberries or go strawberry harvesting to honor the Moon's other correspondences, such as butterflies, frogs, and toads!

Crystals to carry with you: Moonstone or Agate

JULY

Name: Thunder Moon

Zeus, the god-king, is said to have created the universe using thunderbolts in Greek mythology. Thunder and lightning represent immense creative potential and the art of creation. We are being urged to step into our creative talents as we enter the force of the full Thunder Moon on Tuesday, July 19th. What can you do to energize and physically light up your life and the world?

Visualize yourself living your most real and creative life. Allow the image to take over all of your senses and hold it clearly in your thoughts. Break the molds of confinement with the strength and brightness of a rainstorm, and let go of everything that is holding you back from this creation. Have faith in your own abilities.

Alternative name: Buck Moon

The Full Moon in July is known as Buck Moon, in honor of the fresh antlers that appear on deer buck's foreheads at this time. Salmon Moon, Raspberry Moon, and Thunder Moon are some of the other Native American names for it.

Spellwork inspiration: The Thunder Moon is frequently linked to divination. Divination may be done in a variety of methods, and it varies by culture and spirituality. One method to include divination in your Thunder Moon ceremony is to practice tarot, which many witches already do on the Full Moon. Consider asking questions about your own feelings and ideas, as well as any activities you may need to do during the next lunar cycle. Invoke more wisdom and spiritual power by lighting a purple candle.

Crystals to carry with you: Carnelian, Green Calcite, or Yellow Jasper

AUGUST
Name: Herb Moon
The Herb Moon, the first harvest (wheat), and the Lammas sabbat all fall in August. Harvest your herbs now for magical, culinary, and medical purposes throughout the following twelve months. Herbs harvested during this month's waxing and waning phases are more effective than those harvested at any other period of the year. You are balanced between the growth and the enormous reaping on this full moon night. Any herb-based magic will be exceptionally potent. Use the ogham, often known as the tree alphabet, or tea leaves to perform divination.

Alternative name: Dispute Moon
Because of the abundance of Lake Sturgeon in the Great Lakes and Lake Champlain, August is known as the Full Sturgeon Moon. The fish was vital to the local Native American tribes.

It was known to the Celts as Dispute Moon and Lynx Moon.

Spellwork inspiration: There are a variety of rituals and spells that you may utilize under the Herb Moon to help you find equilibrium. Making a healing sachet or an anti-anxiety spell jar now could be a good idea. Fill a yellow pouch with salt, dried lavender, chamomile, and common sage, Citrine, and a piece of paper containing what you'd like to heal or balance, or a healing spell, for healing. Fill a jar with Moon water from the Herb Moon, salt, lavender oil, Amethyst, thyme, and rosemary or basil to help with anxiety.

Crystals to carry with you: Carnelian, Fire Agate, or Citrine

SEPTEMBER
NAME: The Harvest Moon
The Harvest Moon is the full moon in September. This month also marks the second harvest (root crops) and the Mabon sabbat / autumn equinox. This is a particularly busy month for spell-

casters. Cast prosperity spells during the waxing moon phase to secure a plentiful crop. Work magic to improve your health and strength on the night of the full moon. You must prepare for the impending winter by fortifying yourself throughout the harvest, the busiest period of the year. The declining moon phase can be utilized to exorcise any negative energy that may be affecting your crop or endeavors.

Alternative name: Vine Moon
September is the month of the vine, which the Celts called Muin. The vine itself is like a green fuse, rapidly emerging from the Mother. Each species of vine has its own energy viewpoint, whether it's fast growing, prolific, or deeply related to anything it touches. For example, poison ivy is not the same as a grape vine. They do, however, share a certain vigor and fecundity.

Because of the grape, the vine was immensely important in ancient mythology. Wine has been produced for thousands of years and was formerly regarded a very sacred material to be used in rituals, as it is being done in the Catholic mass today. Wine was once associated with theater and a transforming ritual.

Spellwork inspiration: The Harvest Moon is an excellent time to conduct gratitude rituals, which may be as simple as lighting a candle and making a list of all the things for which you are grateful. It may also be the ideal opportunity to perform kitchen witchery and share a meal with someone for whom you are grateful. There's always some type of enchantment to be had in the house, whether you're wanting to make a wholesome, therapeutic dinner or you prefer drinks. To express some of the Harvest Moon's herbal correspondences, cook using wheat or rye.

Crystals to carry with you: Citrine or Peridot

OCTOBER

Name: Blood Moon

The Blood Moon, also known as the Hunter's Moon, occurs in October. This month, harvesting gives place to hunting in order to save enough food for the winter, and the Blood Moon serves as a reminder of the deep link that exists between people and animals. It's an excellent time to perform protection, healing, and blessing magic for your pets and livestock, as well as to figure out what animal energies you require in your own life. Consider going on a shamanic journey to the underworld to meet your spirit animal or to find one to work with.

Alternative name: Shedding Moon

the Moon, when deer shed their antlers and begin the rut, a powerful urge to generate new life that triumphs over winter's death

Spellwork inspiration: Under the full Blood Moon, you can try to connect with the spirit world, but this isn't for everyone though it can be highly gratifying for some. If it isn't your thing, you can make an altar to remember people who have died away. You can decorate the altar with images and artifacts of loved ones, as well as flowers like marigolds (which are associated with both the Harvest Moon and All Hallow's Eve/The Day of the Dead). Others may want to connect with the Hunter's Moon's energy in other ways, such as requesting their ancestors to appear in a tarot spread or just reflecting on the past.

Crystals to carry with you: Obsidian, Turquoise, or Black Tourmaline

NOVEMBER

Name: Mourning Moon

The Mourning Moon arrives in November. Depending on where you reside, it's also known as the Fog Moon or Beaver Moon. Some Native American tribes simply called it The Moon When

Deer Shed Antlers. Use the beauty of this moon phase to celebrate new beginnings if you perceive this month as the start of a new year.

This is a moment for letting go of old baggage and letting go of what no longer serves us. After that, you'll be free to concentrate on the pleasures of the future. Say farewell to unhealthy habits and poisonous relationships during the Mourning Moon phase, and make a fresh start for the new year. Work on improving and deepening your relationship with Deity. Use this month, which follows Samhain, to embrace the darkness and lament or grieve in your own way for things you've lost this year. Allow yourself to relax and unwind.

Alternative name: Beaver Moon
The November Full Moon is named after beavers, who may be observed getting ready for the winter. It was also known as the Frost Moon or Freezing Moon by Native Americans.

It's also known as the Mourning Moon or the Darkest Depths Moon in Celtic mythology.
Spellwork inspiration: While banishing is a strong spell, the lunar eclipse on the Mourning moon might be the ideal occasion to use it. You may be able to spot specific negative energy that is causing a major impediment in your life or a bad habit you're attempting to stop. Many people may write down the energy they desire to expel and then burn it in a fire. Others may opt to bury their list of forbidden items. While there are other banishing rituals to do in conjunction with burning or burying your list, pepper is a tried and tested herb that correlates to banishment and also corresponds to this Moon.

Crystals to carry with you: Lapis Lazuli or Turquoise

DECEMBER

Name: Long Nights Moon

The Long Nights Moon in December, also known as the Cold Moon or Big Winter Moon depending on where you reside, is the last moon phase of the year. As you review the difficulties and tribulations you've faced throughout the previous year, this is frequently a time of reflection and self-discovery. This self-analysis, on the other hand, has a clear benefit: it allows you to re-evaluate where you want to go and who you want to be in the future year. This is a season of transition and adaptability. This is also a time of sharing one's blessings with those less fortunate in many magical traditions, and particularly due to its proximity to Yule and Christmas.

Because this is a dormant season for many of us, the charm of December generally centers on self-discovery and change. We enable ourselves to share our blessings with people around us as we analyze who and what we have become and desire to become and distribute our good fortune and best wishes.

Alternative name: Oak Moon

December's full moon was historically known as the 'Oak Moon,' as it was the first full moon following the Winter Solstice and the last full moon of the year. It was a period when Celtic Druid priests revered the holy Oak tree for its durability and noble presence as a symbol of strength and eternity, and offered ceremonial sacrifices to the gods to request the Oak's immense power, in order to secure survival and lessen the burden of surviving through the harsh winter months.

Spellwork inspiration: The night of the Cold Moon is ideal for writing lists. For focus, light candles and myrrh incense, and compose a list of all you've learnt over the last twelve moon cycles, as well as express gratitude for everything you've accomplished and your manifested dreams. Then, put down your intentions for the upcoming moon cycles, your objectives, and the things you wish to materialize. You may keep it or burn it, just like a wish, and know that whatever you're looking for will find you.

Consider treating yourself to a ceremonial bath with Epsom salts, diluted rosemary oil, and herbs like lavender and chamomile for happiness and tranquility, since the Cold Moon is all about conjuring energy for the long winter ahead. To summon some of the Cold Moon's magical correspondences, find a way to include cranberries, cinnamon, and clove into your daily routine.

Crystals to carry with you: Obsidian, Serpentine, or Smoky Quartz

Animals & Moon Symbolism

The gravitational pull of the Moon has a significant impact on tidal waters, weather, the Earth, and all living things. However, some animals have more symbolic links to the earth's satellite than others. All aquatic organisms have strong Moon connections since the Moon influences water and relates to the same element.

The Feminine Moon has symbolic links to all nocturnal creatures. Animals like the Wolf, Bat, and Black Cat, which are all more active at night and metaphorically connected with the mysterious, occult, and all things concealed, are among the most prominent animal-moon connections. Rabbits have Moon associations as well; the Hare is a global fertility symbol, and some think it appears on the Moon's surface as an optical illusion.

CRAB: The crab is a moon symbol, and it represents water and Cancer in the Zodiac. After watching a creature's physical qualities or activities during and around the full or new moon phase, many people establish animal-moon correlations. The Horseshoe Crab, for example, boosts its spawning activity throughout both moon phases when the tides are at their highest; the Crab is mostly a night breeder and will breed more during the Full and New Moon.

OWLS: When the Moon is full, some owl species, such as the Eagle Owl, become more active. Eagle Owls use the white feathers around their throat to communicate with other birds at night, with the Moon's illumination making the feathers easier to see. On the other hand, some Owls remain dormant during the full moon phase to escape predator attacks. Owls are symbolic of wisdom, secrecy, and the mysterious.

TURTLE: Some critters that can travel on land and sea time their activities to coincide with the Full Moon's arrival. While the Moon reaches its peak, at least some Turtle species lay eggs, making it easier to reach remote portions of the sandy shoreline when riding into land on the waves created by the high tide. Turtles stand for the soil, as well as protection, stability, and perseverance.

DOLPHINS: Because dolphins are both nocturnal and aquatic, they are an obvious Animal-Moon match. During the Full Moon, when the sky is illuminated, the creature forages for food at night. Dolphins, on the other hand, utilize echolocation less frequently, indicating that their habits are tied to the moon cycle. Dolphins represent compassion, insight, wisdom, and the child inside

Moon Numerology

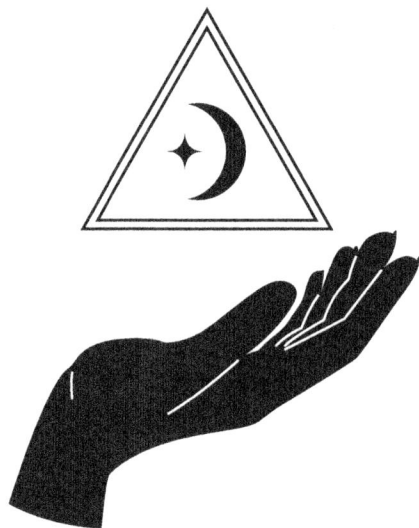

The significance of the Moon becomes much more evident while studying numerology. Every number associated with the Moon has a certain frequency. The vibrations shape and change the symbolic meaning of the Moon, as well as impact the objects it governs in subtle ways. The numbers two, three, four, and twelve all have something to do with the moon.

TWO: The Moon is the second most powerful celestial body, second only to the Sun in terms of influencing the earth and all living things. The good sentiments linked with the number two include balance, solidarity, unity, and duality. Two energies commonly work together: Think about the Yin/Yang forces. The figure also represents diversity and conflict. Codependence, discontent, or struggle are all represented by the number two. Monday gets its name from the Moon, which is considered the second day of the week in many cultures.

THREE: The Blue Moon is the second full Moon of the lunar cycle, which means the Full and New Moons will appear three times in 29 days. The Blue Moon is the second full moon and the third "complete" appearance of the satellite in the night sky, and it relates to the numbers two and three. The Moon also resonates with the number three since each month has at least one full Moon.

Hope, fulfillment, femininity, Divine guidance, and creativity are all represented by the number three. It also sends forth vibrations of enlightenment and vision. Because a Blue Moon is an uncommon occurrence, it is thought to indicate unique possibilities, the unexpected, and a more potent phase for manifesting one's aspirations. Psychic experiences and significant dreams are becoming more common. On the negative side, the Blue Moon's relationship to the number three says that its influence might lead to a lack of focus, confusion, and muddled emotions.

FOUR: When there are thirteen full moons in a given year (13 = 1 + 3 = 4), the Moon aligns with the number four. The number four is connected with strength, stability, balance, and dependability. On the downside, the number four is linked to worry, apprehension of bad luck, tetraphobia (fear of the number four's influence or importance), and insecurity.

EIGHT: While the Moon is commonly thought to have three phases: waxing, full, and waning, it really has eight phases as it moves across the sky. Some of the traits are New, Waxing, First Quarter, Waxing Gibbous, Full, Waning Gibbous, Third Quarter, and Waning. The number eight is related with interconnectedness, rebirth, life lessons, karma, and Heavenly connection or intervention. The number eight is associated with fragility, rigidity, egotism, withdrawal, and a refusal to trust your intuition in a negative meaning.

The Moon & the Tarot

The Tarot is a 78-card divinatory deck that individuals use to examine the past, present, and future, as well as for self-discovery, spiritual pursuits, and life betterment. The Moon and The High Priestess are two cards that deal with the Full Moon and its effects on events, situations, and relationships.

THE MOON: When upright, the Major Arcana's nineteenth card From June 21 through July 22nd, the Moon represents the start of the summer season: Cancer. Two dogs stand at a crossroads on the card, suggesting long-term commitments, forward planning, and the quest of happiness. The Moon and Sun emerge in the sky together, signifying the planetary bodies' united vitality and complete harmony. The secrets, a spiritual journey leading to a stronger connection to the Divine Feminine, motherhood, nurture, compassion, and amorous desires are all symbols on the card. The reverse of the card denotes a lack of ambiguity, things "carved in stone," the realm of tangible logic or rationality, and intellectual pursuits dominate spiritual advancement.

THE HIGH PRIESTESS: The relationship between the High Priestess archetype and moon symbols is less clear than in The Moon Card. The High Priestess, the second card in the Major Arcana, wears a gown that resembles water, has an equal-armed cross over her heart, and a triple moon diadem on her head: a waxing, full, and waning moon crown. She represents feminine secrets, all-world wisdom, intuition, and psychic experiences. The High Priestess, when reversed, denotes a mismatch of mind, body, and soul, or a preference for materialism over the spiritual and emotional realms.

Moon Spells & Rituals

Moon Water

Moon water is water that has been exposed to moonlight and absorbed some of its energy. It may be used for a variety of purposes, including drinking, bathing, and even watering houseplants. Here's how to put it together:

1-Pour water into a container. It's preferable to use fresh rainfall, but any water will suffice.

2-Place your container in the direct light of the moon. It makes no difference whether it's on your doorstep or on a ledge inside! Anywhere where there is moonlight will suffice.

3-Say a prayer or an affirmation. Consider how you want to use the moon water and seal your desire with an affirmation or prayer over the jar.

4-Set aside for the night. Leave the jar in the moonlight overnight once your container is in place and your goal is set. Your moon water will be ready to use in the morning!

Crystal Charging

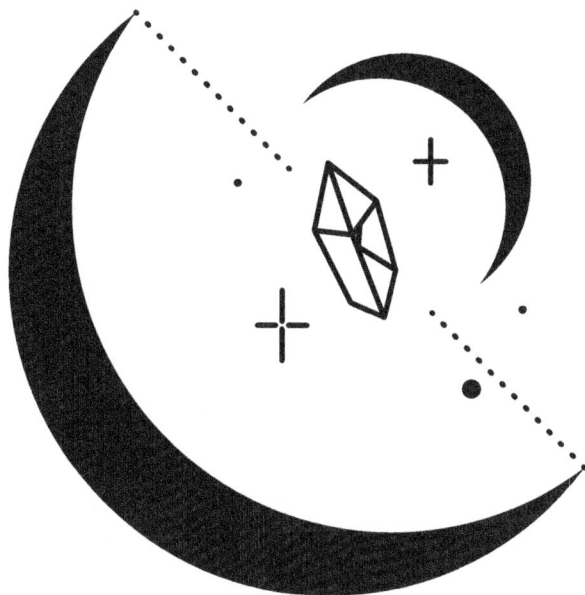

Fill your crystals with energy.

If you're interested in crystals, the full moon is an excellent time to clear and charge them. All you have to do is set your crystals beneath the full moon's rays, much like moon water (inside or outside). You could even mix your crystals with your moon water and use one stone to kill two birds.

Moon Bath

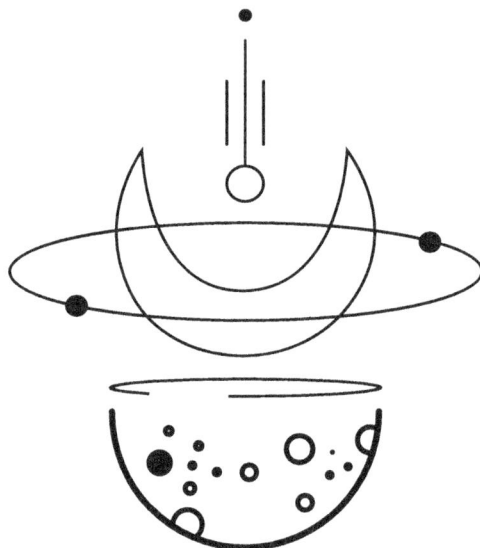

Take a bath under the full moon.
You may light candles that correspond to the colors of the
moon's sign. Submerging oneself in water is a terrific method to
connect with lunar energy.

You may recite your full moon goals aloud while resting in the
tub as you visualize the full moon repairing every cell of your
body, if the weather and location allow, you can even take a
swim in a lake, ocean, or pool.

Moon Manifestation Ritual

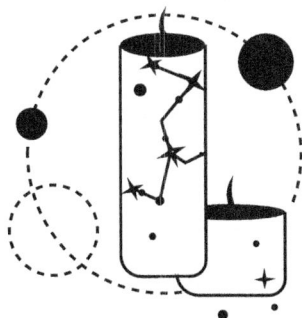

Consider doing a full moon manifestation ritual.
Whatever you're trying to materialize, the full moon can assist
speed things along. A simple manifestation ceremony will help
you cement your full moon intentions and make them a reality.

To get you started, here's one:

1-In your house, make an altar or a holy location where you may
execute this ceremony.

2-Collect some motivational items (photos, notes, books, crystals,
or anything that contains the energy of what you want to manifest).

3-Meditate and quiet your thoughts for a few seconds in front of
your altar while you get clear on what you're calling in.

4-Set aside any judgments and close your eyes while seeing yourself attracting exactly what you desire. The objects can be used as
focal points.

Self-Love Moon Ritual

Make a self-love ritual for yourself.

There's never a terrible moment to practice self-love, but the full moon night is especially magical. This can take the form of almost anything that makes you feel appreciated.

1-Begin the process by doing anything that will help you relax, such as stretching, breathing, or taking a full moon bath.

2-Sit in front of a mirror with a cleansing water of your choosing (moon water, rose water, Florida water, etc.).

3-Using your water, wipe off the mirror with the goal of clearing away any and all illusions that are preventing you from truly loving yourself, allowing yourself to be loved, and uniting with love.

4-Sit in front of a mirror and look at yourself tenderly. You may also use this time to conduct some breathing exercises or recite a mantra anything that helps you connect to your heart.

5-Thank yourself, the moon, and the cosmos for keeping you in self-love at the end of the ceremony.

Waxing Moon Hair Growth Spell

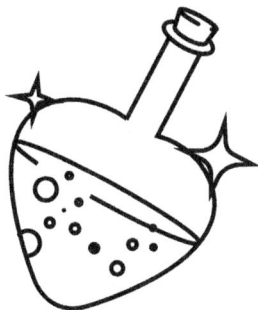

Aids in the quicker, stronger, and healthier growth of your hair.

For this Waxing Moon, you'll require:

Moon water from the waxing moon
Clear intention
The first night of the waxing moon

1-While you're rinsing your hair with the moon water, chant

"Waxing moon, beautiful moon Let my hair grow strong with the waxing of the moon, beyond my chin down to my knees, since this is my desire, so let it be."

2-Envision your hair being the length and thickness you desire, then imagine it growing and becoming that way.

3-Repeat every night until the full moon arrives; you may also perform this on the full moon's night, but that is entirely up to you.

Moon Love Ritual

Make a love ritual for the full moon.
Use a honey jar magic to attract love during this full moon.
you'll require:

Honey, Alcohol of your choice in a tiny jar (vodka, rum, tequila, etc.)
To express love with healthy boundaries, use rose petals and thorns.
Herbs that are associated with love (think blue lotus for an aphrodisiac, lavender for healing, cinnamon for lust, patchouli for passion, oregano for good luck, and so on)
A rose quartz crystal
A pen and a sheet of paper
A candle

1-In a jar, combine a little honey and your alcohol, as well as your rose petals and thorns, herbs, and crystal.

2-Place a piece of paper in the jar with your purpose written in the past or present tense (not future tense), such as "I found a lover."

3-Close the lid and shake it vigorously while picturing your goal.

4-Light a candle and declare your objective to the cosmos and full moon, imagining what it would be like to achieve it.

5-Raise energy levels by singing, dancing or playing drums, for example.

6-Place the candle in the sink to burn out. Take a time to mentally close out the ritual when it's finished burning, thanking the cosmos, moon, and/or any deities you work with.

7-Knowing that your spell is complete, throw the jar in a garbage can at a crossroads (the modern-day crossroads, where witches originally hid items).

Lunar Blessing

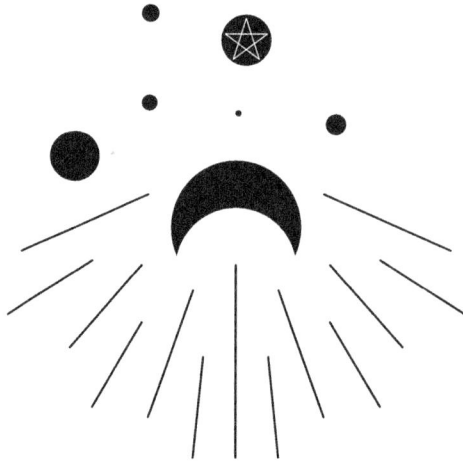

This spell can only be performed when the moon is full.

Perform this activity outside, where you can see the moon.
Find a natural setting to execute your magic.
If possible, you should be able to see the moon or be in a position to receive its energy.

This spell will require the following items:

1 candle, white

1-Step outdoors into the moonlight light your candle and say

"Oh, Great Moon, provide me protection and blessings. x 3
Oh, Full Moon, provide me power and the capacity to live in peace. x 3
Oh, Bright Moon, provide me grace and luck x 3

So mote it be x 3"

Release Spell for the Full Moon

Light a candle.

It is recommended to use a basic tea light candle for this; if you have the time to let the candle burn completely, it will be a very strong spell.

Find out what you want to materialize for this moon cycle, as well as what you may let go of that no longer serves you.

1-Set your purpose when you light your flame. Say it as clearly as you can, out loud or in your brain, leaving no space for interpretation.

Moon Wish Spell

This spell takes some time to accomplish and necessitates a significant amount of time spent in contemplation.

This spell will require the following items:

Five silver candles
A colored candle of your choice

1-Clear your thoughts of all clutter or concentrate for a brief period of time to ensure that your wishes have been defined. Place the silver candles in a pentagram form where they may safely burn. Start at the top and ignite them according to the pentagram's connecting lines.
As you do so say:

"Moon above, which shines so brightly, guard my deep slumber tonight, I pray to you with this plea My life unfolds at my command."

2-Allow at least half an hour for the candles to burn before turning them out and preparing for sleep. Light the other candle the next morning and meditate or reflect on your wishes for another thirty minutes. Spend some time imagining how your life would be when your wishes come true. Rep this process for the following three evenings.

3-Ultimately, on the fourth morning, relight all of the candles and let them burn out while playing some inspiring music. Consider your wishes in the last hour, while the candles are still burning, and make any alterations that seem reasonable.

Writing Manifestation Moon Spell

This magic permits you to be as imaginative as you want; your imagination will be the spell's fuel, so go as crazy as you want.

What you will need:

A piece of paper or notebook
A candle

1-Write down anything that comes to mind based on your objectives on a piece of paper or in a notebook.
If you're an artist, draw your perfect life, and if you prefer to be organized, write a list.

Create your best expression of how you want your life to be, even if it's wacky, on the paper.

If you're looking to heal, describe what your recovery process looks like on this page.

2-Fold the paper towards you 2 times then stop then 1 times again.

3-Place the paper under a candle and allow the candles to burn so that its wax covers the paper but do not burn it.

1-Throw it away on the Waning Crescent Moon.

Grounding Moon Spell

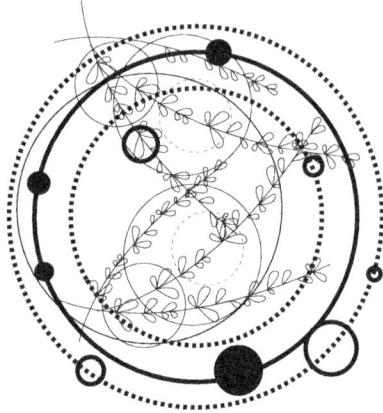

1-Remove your shoes and place your feet on the ground out-side.

Take note of how the soil feels beneath your feet and how safe you feel on the ground.

2-Keep your breathing steady. Even simply listening to a meditation music might be beneficial.

3-Thank the moon for its vitality, and thank whoever you prayed to when you're finished.

4-Take a breath and center yourself. Allow yourself to complete this release at this time.

You have the right to your feelings, and you have the right to grieve the grief you are experiencing.
Tears can be energy that is leaving your body.

5-Give in and trust that what is best for you will arrive.

Financial Blessing Full Moon Spell

See a positive impact in your finances.

For this spell, you'll need the following item:

Money made of paper

1-From the new moon to the full moon, locate the moon in the sky...if feasible, stand outside and place the paper money in each hand.

2-Repeat the following chant 3 times:

"Moon, Moon, oh Moon, oh wonderful Moon... Fairer than any star.
If that is so, Moon, oh Moon, bring me money and prosperity...
So will it be."

Money Spell for the Full Moon

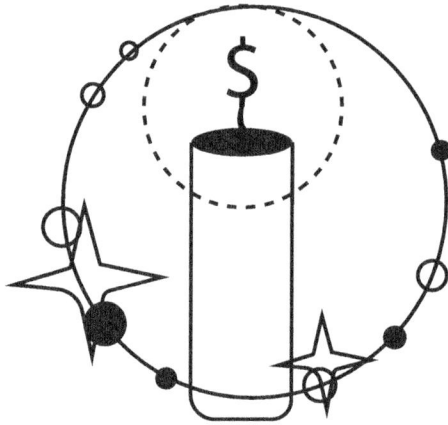

With the power of the full moon, you may attract fortune.

This spell will require the following items:

Green Candle
Sandalwood oil/Patchouli

1-Carve your name on the green candle. If desired, anoint it with Patchouli or Sandalwood essential oil. Recite the following mantra while doing so:

"The moment has come for me to weave my will.
I bring the strength of the moon inside me to wield it.
I sent out my energy into the cosmos to manifest my desired outcome."

2-Turn on your candle. Recite this mantra while focusing on the energies being thrown into it and turned into power as they escape via the smoke and flames to fulfill your bidding:

"Grant me my desire tonight, full moon dazzling, full moon's brilliance.
Bring lasting prosperity into my life, and all my difficulties will fade away.
Allow money to flow to me right now.
So let it be, with no harm to anyone."

3-Allow the candle to naturally burn out.

Love Spell for the Full Moon

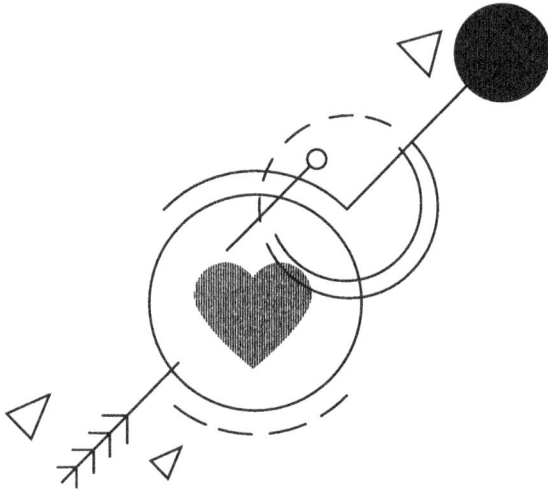

This spell will require the following items:

Meditation-Energy
Full Moon
Herbs-Basil and Cinnamon
Candle-Pink
Rose quarts to increase the spell.
Paper or Parchment Paper and pen

Concentrate your willpower on achieving your goals and ask yourself why do you wish to cast the spell?
Make certain the moon is full.

Anoint your pink candle with the herbs (Basil and Cinnamon), light the pink candle, write on a piece of paper "(your name or someone else's name) and then put the targets name on top of your own or someone else's name" the spell may be done for a buddy.

Visualize your objective being achieved and the two individuals you've selected being united within the flame. To boost the candle's energy, create a crystal grid around it.
Then repeat this chant 3 times:

"With the power of these plants and stones, I pray to combine these two souls so that they may find happiness, and may their romance combined kindle the affections of themselves and others. So it shall be".

Wish Upon the Full Moon Spell

For this spell, you'll need the following item:

1 Glass of Juice/Wine

Go outside with a drink at night beneath a full moon. Look up at the moon and tell her anything you want, imagining your wish coming true. Be descriptive and as detailed as possible. Lift your glass in a salute to the moon, and say, with additional visualisation of the wish coming true:

"Oh moon spirit, have a look at this goblet I present thee; it is yours for everything that you do, gracious one of silver color."

Pour your drink into the earth, expecting that your wish would come true.

Lunar Eclipse Spell

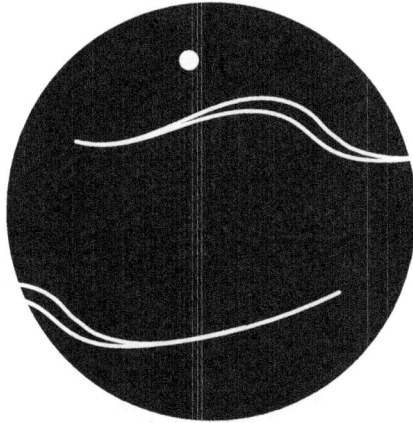

The moon eclipse's power is summoned in this magic to bestow one wish or power. The spell should be used only on eclipses of the Moon.

1-Prepare your mind by meditating.

2-While taking a ritualistic bath, meditate. Believe that as you drain the water, all of the negative from that day disappears with it.

3-Then, a few minutes before the eclipse, walk outdoors and select a safe spot where you can plainly view the moon.

4-"I call the spirit of the eclipsed moon with its faces and shapes," declare when the moon is entirely eclipsed. "I call upon its might and beseech thee to grant me a request. I wish I will (say wish here, be explicit). I am grateful to you, Great Moon. So shall it be, as I will"

Moon Power Spell

Because this magic is an invocation to the Moon, it is quite easy. Apart from a physical depiction of the Moon, not much further instruments or procedures are required.

For this spell, you'll need the following items:

A bowl of water
White flower

Place the flower in the bowl and let it float. Raise the bowl to the Moon in the sky and recite:

"Hail to thee, river's white swan. Lady of tides. All hail moving through the streams of existence. Mother of the past and future, We cling to your aura this night, to you, via you. I am in your strength and knowledge, pure reflection, absolute belief, touched by your presence. Praise your might, your tranquility, my might, my tranquility. I am a powerful individual. I salute you. I praise. I bless."

On the altar, replace the bowl. Consider how powerful the Moon is for a few seconds. The Moon considers water to be holy, therefore we present it to her.

SPELL OF THE SNOW MOON

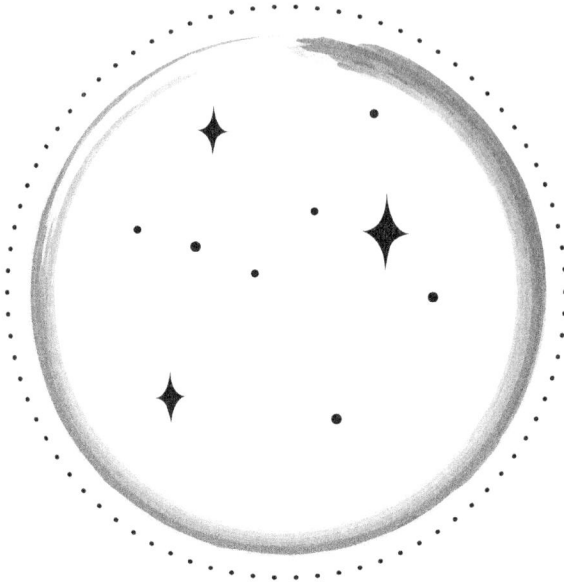

You may ask the Snow Moon to help you make positive changes in your life around the time of the Snow Moon. You can awaken to a new purpose or calling, just as nature is about to emerge from its winter slumber.

This is a very straightforward spell for reawakening a new purpose or calling.

You will need the following items for this spell:

The full moon of the snow moon
a violet candle

Declare your magical goals to the Snow Moon on the night of the Snow Moon. As a thank you, light a violet candle and say to her as follows:

"As the Earth wraps itself in a white cocoon,
Snow Moon, you protect the night in frosty splendor.
Allow me to change, to be reborn; now I plant the miraculous
seed; I am reborn."

Keep your candle burning until it extinguishes on its own.

Moon Ring Spell

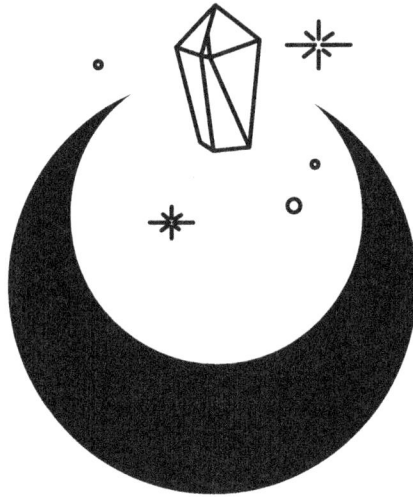

This spell creates a moon ring that harnesses the power of the moon to grant you supernatural abilities.

For this spell, you'll need the following items:

A blue gemstone is set in a ring.

On a full moon, go outside, put on the ring, and point it at the moon. After that, say the spell out loud.

"I summon the moon's rays to provide me its power. To only utilize my abilities for good and never to hurt people. You perceive me now as ordinary, but that will change shortly when I summon the moon's rays. Give me the full moon's strength."

Keep the ring on and recharge the spell when you can. When the sun rises, your abilities will rise with it.

Candle Ritual for Setting Intentions During an Eclipse

To express your objectives, this ceremony employs a little candle magic. You'll need one candle that can burn for seven days and that you can carve into. The hue should match your aims, and if you're unsure, white is always a good choice.

1-Make a list of three new items you'd want to include in your life throughout this lunar cycle. A new career, a romance, an apartment, and so on are examples of these.

2-Make an affirmation that corresponds to your new list of goals.

3-Prepare your candle. Remember that you may choose the hue based on your objective. If you're feeling very inventive, carve your name and your affirmation onto the candle. If you're into aesthetics, you may also add some scent oil and glitter.

4-As you light your candle, repeat your affirmation three times.

5-Imagine yourself living your affirmation for a few seconds. Consider as many details as possible.

6-Every day, repeat Steps 4 and 5 until the candle burns out on its own.

7-Keep an eye on the miracle unfolding.

Meditation for Eclipse Release

During a full moon eclipse, this soothing meditation may be utilized to help you let go of any undesirable habits, unpleasant individuals, or unfavorable circumstances that no longer benefit you. To complete this final ceremony, all you need is a quiet area, a little creativity, and 10 minutes.

1-Close your eyes and sit in a quiet place in a comfortable position.

2-Allow your heart rate to gradually fall by taking a couple of deep breaths in through the nose and out through the mouth.

3-Imagine floating through the sky towards the moon, lifting up and out of your body. It's very vital to trust your imagination at this point. Don't pass judgment on whether or not your imagination tries to fly; simply go with it.

4-Take a walk around the moon after you've arrived in your imagination.

5-Imagine you've spotted a woman dressed entirely in white approaching you. She's one of the moon's emissaries, and she's come to relay a message to you.

6-Inquire with her about what the full moon eclipse wants you to let go of in order to reach your full potential, and why now is the best time. Listen attentively and without passing judgment.

7-Imagine a manifestation of what you'd like to let go of emerging beside the moon lady. It may appear in whatever way you want it to. It may be your boss if it's a job. It might be your past spouse if you have a negative relationship habit.

8-You glance down to find a black cord linking you to the habit as the moon lady takes out a gorgeous selenite sword. She ponders as to whether or not she is ideal for cutting it.

9-You envision the knife slicing the rope and reducing it to ash as you nod. You hug the moon representative, who expresses her pride in you.

10-Allow yourself time to return to your body when the ceremony is over.

11-When you're ready, spend a few moments to jot down as many facts as you can in case you need them later.

Full Moon Eclipse Smudging & Protection Ritual

This ritual requires four pieces of black tourmaline, a feather, and incense you can burn such as palo santo, sage, lavender, mugwort, or frankincense. It will help to release any yucky energy trapped in your home that may have been leftover from previous houseguests, or even the last time you were in a bad mood. This ritual is best performed during a Full Moon Eclipse.

1-To begin, ignite your smudge stick. Start from one room in your house and go past every wall, allowing the smoke to drift into each space once it's producing a healthy volume of smoke. Direct the smoke with your feather, paying great attention to windows and doors.

2-While directing the smoke, say aloud, "All that does not belong here, depart immediately, thank you very much."

3-Repetition is required in every part of the house.

4-Smudge your body once you've smudged every room. Begin with your head, directing the smoke with the feather to get the soles of your feet.

5-Allow the smoke to soak each piece of black tourmaline before proceeding. You may use your smudge stick once your tourmaline is pristine.

6-Create a large crystal grid by placing your black tourmaline at the four corners of your home. Try to arrange them in a symmetrical pattern.

7-Once they're in place, ask the universe to guard your home's energy and keep anything that isn't connected with your greater purpose out.

Other Moon Correspondences

Moon Deities

Selene, Sophia, Thoth, Artemis, Diana, Luna, Blodeuwedd, Man in the Moon, Rabbit in the Moon, Khonsu, Inanna, Hecate, Cerridwen, Coyolxauhqui, Sina, Gabriel, Mani, Morgan Le Fay, Cliodhna

Herb, Vegetable, and Fruit Correspondences of the Moon

NEW MOONS:

- Cabbage

- Lettuce

- Kale

- Spinach

- Cucumber

- Cauliflower

- Mint

- Basil

- Oregano

- Angelica

- Ginger

- Lavender

WAXING GIBBOUS MOONS:

- Bean   - Dill

- Lintel   - Coriander

- Blueberry   - Saff lower

- Blackberry   - Hyssop

- Tomatoe   - Parsley

- Squash   - Clover

THE FULL MOON:

- Corn   - Yarrow

- Onions   - Sage

- Beets   - Dandelion

- Carrots   - Thyme

- Leaks   - Marjoram

- Radish   - Horehound

WAINING GIBBOUS - THIRD QUARTER:

- Lemon

- Orange

- Grape

- Lime

- Strawberry

- Mellisa

- Vanilla

- Myrtle

- Catnip

- Nutmeg

DARK MOONS:

- Walnut

- Almond

- Oak

- Tarragon

- Anise

- Bergamot

Printed in Great Britain
by Amazon